Welcome to the updated version of the USCIS Naturalization Test Study Guide. This is the new version that everyone who has applied for citizenship will receive. The new version contains 100 questions and answers. This study guide is here to help you pass the test. The test is an Oral test, meaning the USCIS officer or agent will be asking you questions verbally and you must respond verbally. And so this book is here to help you be as close to that interview as possible so you can feel confident and succeed. I'll ask you the questions from the test, then you practice answering the question just like the actual interview. Flip the page to see if you were correct. This will help you study.

Ready? Let's begin!

Question 1. What is the supreme law of the land?

the Constitution

Question 2. What does the Constitution do?

Answers include:
sets up the government
defines the government
protects basic rights of Americans

Question 3. The idea of self-government is in the first three words of the Constitution. What are these words?

We the People

Question 4. What is an amendment?

Answers include:
a change (to the Constitution)
an addition (to the Constitution)

Question 5. What do we call the first ten amendments to the
Constitution?

the Bill of Rights

Question 6. What is one right or freedom from the First Amendment?

Answers include:
speech
religion
assembly
press
petition the government

Question 7. How many amendments does the Constitution have?

twenty-seven (27)

Question 8. What did the Declaration of Independence do?

Answers include:
announced our independence (from Great Britain)
declared our independence (from Great Britain)
said that the United States is free (from Great Britain)

Question 9. What are two rights in the Declaration of Independence?

Answers include:
life
liberty
pursuit of happiness

Question 10. What is freedom of religion?

You can practice any religion, or not practice a religion.

Question 11. What is the economic system in the United States?

Answers include:
capitalist economy
market economy

Question 12. What is the "rule of law"?

Answers include:
Everyone must follow the law.
Leaders must obey the law.
Government must obey the law.
No one is above the law.

Question 13. Name one branch or part of the government.

Answers include:
Congress
legislative
President
executive
the courts
judicial

Question 14. What stops one branch of government from becoming too powerful?

Answers include:
checks and balances
separation of powers

29

Question 15. Who is in charge of the executive branch?

the President

Question 16. Who makes federal laws?

Answers include:
Congress
Senate and House (of Representatives)
(U.S. or national) legislature

Question 17. What are the two parts of the U.S. Congress?

the Senate and House (of Representatives)

Question 18. How many U.S. Senators are there?

one hundred (100)

Question 19. We elect a U.S. Senator for how many years?

six (6)

Question 20. Who is one of your state's U.S. Senators now?

Your answer were very. You'll need to look that up depending on your state of residence. If you're in the D. C or District of Columbia and resident there or a resident of a U. S. Territory, you should answer that that territory or that D. C has no senators.

Question 21. The House of Representatives has how many vot-
ing members?

four hundred thirty-five (435)

Question 22. We elect a U.S. Representative for how many years?

two (2)

Question 23. Name your U.S. Representative.

Your answer were very. You'll need to look that up depending on your state of residence. If you're in the D. C or District of Columbia and resident there or a resident of a U. S. Territory, you should answer that that territory or that D. C has no senators.

Question 24. Who does a U.S. Senator represent?

all people of the state

Question 25. Why do some states have more Representatives than other states?

Answers include:
(because of) the state's population
(because) they have more people
(because) some states have more people

Question 26. We elect a President for how many years?

four (4)

Question 27. In what month do we vote for President?

November

Question 28. What is the name of the President of the United States now?

Joe Biden

Question 29. What is the name of the Vice President of the
United States now?

Kamala Harris

Question 30. If the President can no longer serve, who becomes President?

the Vice President

Question 31. If both the President and the Vice President can no longer serve, who becomes President?

the Speaker of the House

63

Question 32. Who is the Commander in Chief of the military?

the President

Question 33. Who signs bills to become laws?

the President

Question 34. Who vetoes bills?

the President

Question 35. What does the President's Cabinet do?

advises the President

Question 36. What are two Cabinet-level positions?

Answers include:
Secretary of Agriculture
Secretary of Commerce
Secretary of Defense
Secretary of Education
Secretary of Energy
Secretary of Health and Human Services
Secretary of Homeland Security
Secretary of Housing and Urban Development
Secretary of the Interior
Secretary of Labor
Secretary of State
Secretary of Transportation
Secretary of the Treasury
Secretary of Veterans Affairs
Attorney General
Vice President

Question 37. What does the judicial branch do?

Answers include:
reviews laws
explains laws
resolves disputes (disagreements)
decides if a law goes against the Constitution

Question 38. What is the highest court in the United States?

the Supreme Court

Question 39. How many justices are on the Supreme Court?

9

Question 40. Who is the Chief Justice of the United States now?

John Roberts

Question 41. Under our Constitution, some powers belong to the federal government. What is one power of the federal government?

Answers include:
to print money
to declare war
to create an army
to make treaties

Question 42. Under our Constitution, some powers belong to the states. What is one power of the states?

Answers include:
provide schooling and education
provide protection (police)
provide safety (fire departments)
give a driver's license
approve zoning and land use

Question 43. Who is the Governor of your state now?

Your answer were very. You'll need to look that up depending on your state of residence.

Question 44. What is the capital of your state?

Your answer were very. You'll need to look that up depending on your state of residence. If you're in the D. C or District of Columbia and resident there or a resident of a U. S. Territory, you should answer that that territory's capital or that D.C. has is not a state and does not have a capital.

Question 45. What are the two major political parties in the
United States?

Republican and Democrat

91

Republican and Democrat

Question 46. What is the political party of the President now?

Democrat

Question 47. What is the name of the Speaker of the House of Representatives now?

Nancy Pelosi

Question 48. There are four amendments to the Constitution about who can vote. Describe one of them.

Answers include:
Citizens eighteen (18) and older (can vote).
You don't have to pay (a poll tax) to vote.
Any citizen can vote. (Women and men can vote.)
A male citizen of any race (can vote).

Question 49. What is one responsibility that is only for United States citizens?

Answers include:
serve on a jury
vote in a federal election

Question 50. Name one right only for United States citizens.

Answers include:
vote in a federal election
run for federal office

Question 51. What are two rights of everyone living in the United States?

Answers include:
freedom of expression
freedom of speech
freedom of assembly
freedom to petition the government
freedom of religion
the right to bear arms

Question 52. What do we show loyalty to when we say the Pledge of Allegiance?

Answers include:
the United States
the flag

Question 53. What is one promise you make when you become a United States citizen?

Answers include:
give up loyalty to other countries
defend the Constitution and laws of the United States
obey the laws of the United States
serve in the U.S. military (if needed)
serve (do important work for) the nation (if needed)
be loyal to the United States

Question 54. How old do citizens have to be to vote for President?

eighteen (18) and older

Question 55. What are two ways that Americans can participate in their democracy?

Answers include:
vote
join a political party
help with a campaign
join a civic group
join a community group
give an elected official your opinion on an issue
call Senators and Representatives
publicly support or oppose an issue or policy
run for office
write to a newspaper

Question 56. When is the last day you can send in federal income tax forms?

April 15

Question 57. When must all men register for the Selective Service?

Answers include:
at age eighteen (18)
between eighteen (18) and twenty-six (26)
AMERICAN HISTORY

Question 58. What is one reason colonists came to America?

Answers include:
freedom
political liberty
religious freedom
economic opportunity
practice their religion
escape persecution

Question 59. Who lived in America before the Europeans arrived?

Answers include:
American Indians
Native Americans

Question 60. What group of people was taken to America and sold as slaves?

Answers include:
Africans
people from Africa

121

Question 61. Why did the colonists fight the British?

Answers include:
because of high taxes (taxation without representation)
because the British army stayed in their houses (boarding, quartering)
because they didn't have self-government

Question 62. Who wrote the Declaration of Independence?

(Thomas) Jefferson

Question 63. When was the Declaration of Independence adopted?

July 4, 1776

Question 64. There were 13 original states. Name three.

Answers include:
New Hampshire
Massachusetts
Rhode Island
Connecticut
New York
New Jersey
Pennsylvania
Delaware
Maryland
Virginia
North Carolina
South Carolina
Georgia

Question 65. What happened at the Constitutional Convention?

Answers include:
The Constitution was written.
The Founding Fathers wrote the Constitution.

Question 66. When was the Constitution written?

1787

Question 67. The Federalist Papers supported the passage of the U.S. Constitution. Name one of the writers.

Answers include:
(James) Madison
(Alexander) Hamilton
(John) Jay
Publius

Question 68. What is one thing Benjamin Franklin is famous for?

Answers include:
U.S. diplomat
oldest member of the Constitutional Convention
first Postmaster General of the United States
writer of "Poor Richard's Almanac"
started the first free libraries

Question 69. Who is the "Father of Our Country"?

(George) Washington

Question 70. Who was the first President?

(George) Washington

Question 71. What territory did the United States buy from France in 1803?

Answers include:
the Louisiana Territory
Louisiana

143

Question 72. Name one war fought by the United States in the 1800s.

Answers include:
War of 1812
Mexican-American War
Civil War
Spanish-American War

Question 73. Name the U.S. war between the North and the South.

Answers include:
the Civil War
the War between the States

147

Question 74. Name one problem that led to the Civil War.

Answers include:
slavery
economic reasons
states' rights

Question 75. What was one important thing that Abraham Lincoln did?

Answers include:
freed the slaves (Emancipation Proclamation)
saved (or preserved) the Union
led the United States during the Civil War

Question 76. What did the Emancipation Proclamation do?

Answers include:
freed the slaves
freed slaves in the Confederacy
freed slaves in the Confederate states
freed slaves in most Southern states

Question 77. What did Susan B. Anthony do?

Answers include:
fought for women's rights
fought for civil rights

Question 78. Name one war fought by the United States in the 1900s.

Answers include:
World War I
World War II
Korean War
Vietnam War
(Persian) Gulf War

Question 79. Who was President during World War I?

(Woodrow) Wilson

Question 80. Who was President during the Great Depression and World War II?

(Franklin) Roosevelt

Question 81. Who did the United States fight in World War II?

Japan, Germany, and Italy

Question 82. Before he was President, Eisenhower was a general. What war was he in?

World War II

Question 83. During the Cold War, what was the main concern
of the United States?

Communism

Question 84. What movement tried to end racial discrimination?

civil rights (movement)

Question 85. What did Martin Luther King, Jr. do?

Answers include:
fought for civil rights
worked for equality for all Americans

Question 86. What major event happened on September 11, 2001, in the United States?

Terrorists attacked the United States.

Question 87. Name one American Indian tribe in the United States.

Answers include:
Cherokee
Navajo
Sioux
Chippewa
Choctaw
Pueblo
Apache
Iroquois
Creek
Blackfeet
Seminole
Cheyenne
Arawak
Shawnee
Mohegan
Huron
Oneida
Lakota
Crow
Teton
Hopi
Inuit

Question 88. Name one of the two longest rivers in the United States.

Answers include:
Missouri (River)
Mississippi (River)

Question 89. What ocean is on the West Coast of the United
States?

Pacific (Ocean)

Question 90. What ocean is on the East Coast of the United
States?

Atlantic (Ocean)

Question 91. Name one U.S. territory.

Answers include:
Puerto Rico
U.S. Virgin Islands
American Samoa
Northern Mariana Islands
Guam

Question 92. Name one state that borders Canada.

Answers include:
Maine
New Hampshire
Vermont
New York
Pennsylvania
Ohio
Michigan
Minnesota
North Dakota
Montana
Idaho
Washington
Alaska

Question 93. Name one state that borders Mexico.

Answers include:
California
Arizona
New Mexico
Texas

Question 94. What is the capital of the United States?

Washington, D.C.

189

Question 95. Where is the Statue of Liberty?

Answers include:
New York (Harbor)
Liberty Island
New Jersey
near New York City

Question 96. Why does the flag have 13 stripes?

Answers include:
because there were 13 original colonies
because the stripes represent the original colonies

Question 97. Why does the flag have 50 stars?

Answers include:
because there is one star for each state
because each star represents a state
because there are 50 states

Question 98. What is the name of the national anthem?

The Star-Spangled Banner

Question 99. When do we celebrate Independence Day?

July 4

Question 100. Name two national U.S. holidays.

Answers include:
New Year's Day
Martin Luther King, Jr. Day
Presidents' Day
Memorial Day
Independence Day
Labor Day
Columbus Day
Veterans Day
Thanksgiving
Christmas

YOU FINISHED!

I want to say great job for getting through these questions. Your goal of becoming a U.S. citizen is in reach. All you need to do is study work hard and have confidence going into the test. Go ahead and practice these questions over a good period of time, so when you have the actual test, you will approach them with confidence. Know that you can do this. My parents have naturalized and become U.S. citizens, and many people do it every single day. If they can do it, you can do it. Good luck!